2023

Vision Board

Words, Clip Art and Picture Book

HONEYBEE PUBLISHING

HOW TO USE YOUR VISION BOARD FOR LIFE-CHANGING MANIFESTATION

1. stare at your vision board. what is calling your attention on that specIfic day?

2. Look at your chosen picture and remember what it means, paying attention to every detail

3. Close your eyes and imagine your life when that specific goal is already your reality. how do you feel? where are you? who is with you?

4. Create a story inside your head, imagining your moves, the conversation, what is happening around you... then, take your time immersing yourself in that story.

5. Take a deep breath in, hold it for four seconds, and slowly release. open your eyes

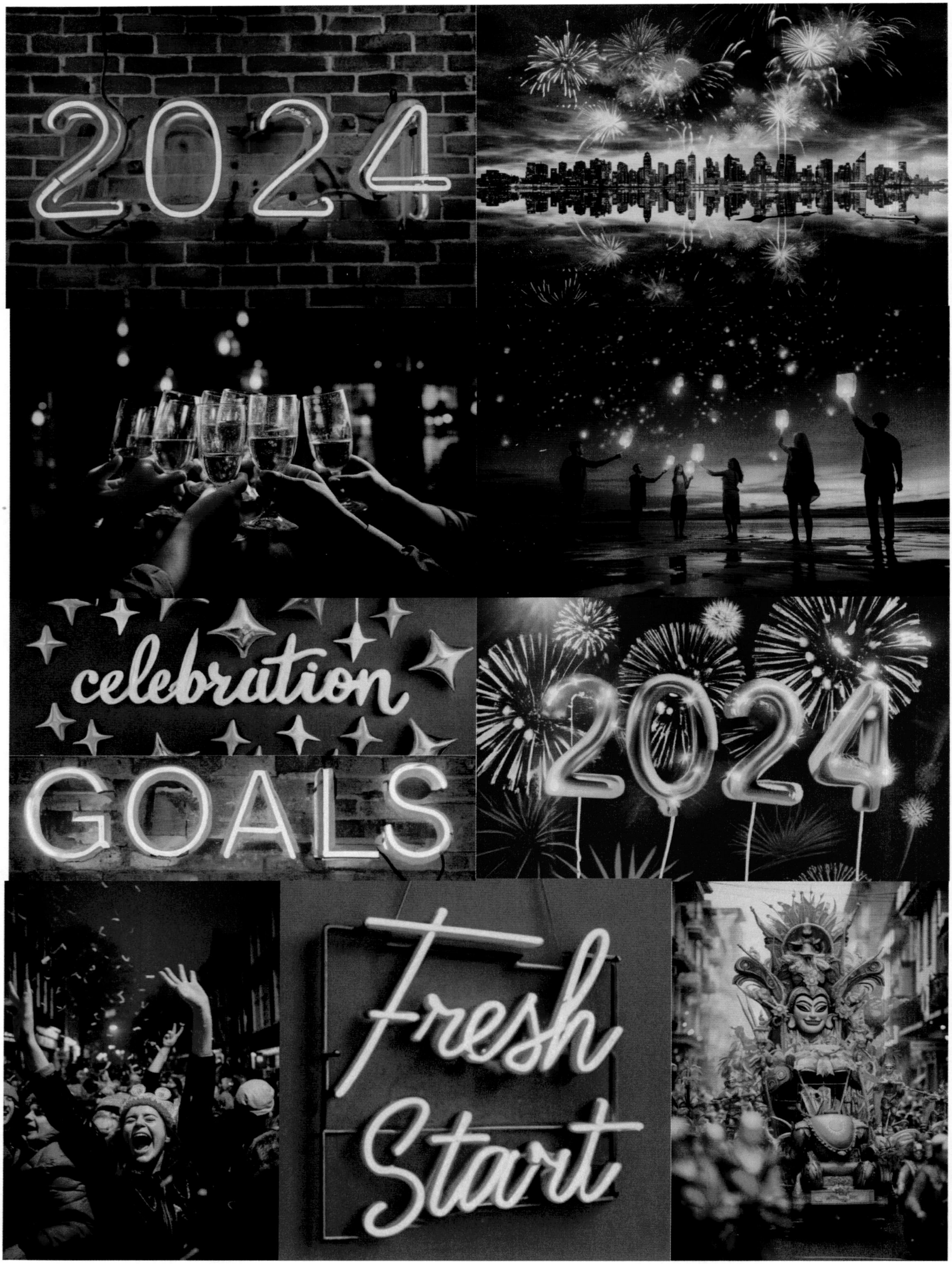
2024
celebration
GOALS
2024
Fresh
Start

CATEGORIES

FAMILY	CAREER
RELATIONSHIP	WEALTH
FRIENDSHIP	HOME
TRAVEL	CAR
HEALTH	FITNESS

GOALS

BABY

FULFILLING CAREER

family time

DO MORE EXERCISE

loving relationship

eat nutrious food

DREAM VACATION

DE-STRESS

new home

NEW CAR

SOULMATE

more friends

LEARN A CRAFT

GET RICH

MORE ME TIME

LEARN A LANGUAGE

DEBT FREE

free from anxiety

read more

love myself

PROMOTION

START BUSINESS

investments

WRITE A BOOK

abundance

DETERMINATION

PATIENCE

LUXURY CRUISE

ART

SEE THE WORLD

FORGIVE

I am creating the life of my dreams

choose JOY

"Pray more, worry less"

BRAVE

CHERISH

family

SPIRITUAL

GOALS

POSITIVE MINDSET

MAKE A DIFFERENCE

YOGA

fitness

PRAY

DANCE

I AM	I AM
I AM	I AM

FREE	growing
resilient	powerful
WEALTHY	content
beautiful	DETERMINED

VACATION

If your dreams don't scare you, they are too small

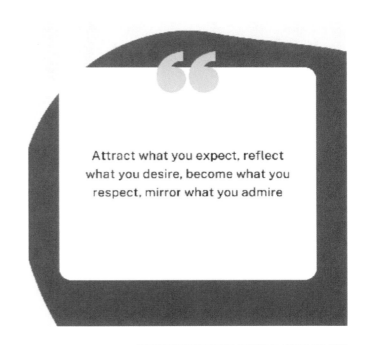

Attract what you expect, reflect what you desire, become what you respect, mirror what you admire

STRIVE FOR PROGRESS, NOT PERFECTION

GOOD MORNING QUOTES

Anything is possible if you have enough nerve

6AM Success

Give yourself the gift of freedom, of being open to what is to come

A beautiful day begins with a beautiful mindset

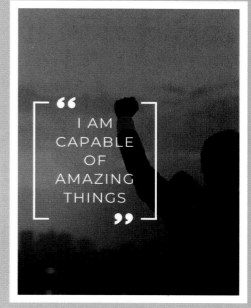

I AM
CAPABLE
OF
AMAZING
THINGS

Eat according
to your goals

YOUR
BODY
ACHIEVES
WHAT
YOUR
MIND
BELIEVES

nourish

GRACE

self-care

STRENGTH

entrepreneur

confidence

indurance

HAPPY

stay focussed

read more

side hussle

I AM	I AM
I AM	I AM

loved	confident
at peace	successful
HEALTHY	FIT
worthy	HAPPY

Go on, write yourself a check - **you deserve it!**

BANK OF THE UNIVERSE
1 MANIFESTATION AV.
LAW OF ATTRACTION CITY

Date: _____

Pay _____

_____

_____ Dollars

$

For _____

The Giver of Everything

AUTHORIZED SIGNATURE

0123456 789 87654321   0123456 789 87654321

In the mood to do some travelling? Write yourself a boarding pass!

✈ UNIVERSAL AIRLINES   Boarding Pass   Boarding Pass

Passenger Name   Flight   Seat   Passenger Name
                        AB 1234   15A

From   Date   Gate   From
To   A5   To

                        Boarding Time   Flight   Seat   Gate
0 1 2 3 4 5 6 7 8 9   10:00 AM   AB 1234   15A   A5

                                                    Boarding Time
                                                    10:00 AM

We cannot become who we want by remaining who we are

Don't compare your life to others. There is no comparison between the sun and the moon - they shine when it's their time.

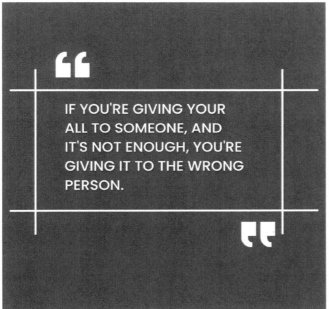
IF YOU'RE GIVING YOUR ALL TO SOMEONE, AND IT'S NOT ENOUGH, YOU'RE GIVING IT TO THE WRONG PERSON.

Be the reason someone smiles today

Two things you are in total control of in life are your attitude and your effort

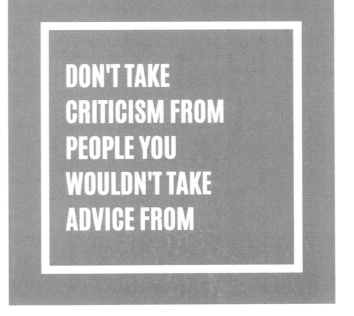
DON'T TAKE CRITICISM FROM PEOPLE YOU WOULDN'T TAKE ADVICE FROM

Think it,
want it,
get it
———

IF YOU ARE
waiting
FOR THE
RIGHT TIME
IT'S **NOW**

DO
MORE OF
WHAT
YOU
LOVE.

believe

LOVE

abundance

Heal

play

BALANCE

billionaire

HEALTHY

calm

TRAVEL

energy

I AM	I AM
I AM	I AM

- fill in the blanks -

healthy

eat your greens

nourished

HYDRATED

EAT MORE VEG

energised

radiant

VIBRANT

"

You are so much
stronger than you
think

- *Daily Reminder* -

WHAT GOOD ARE
WINGS

WITHOUT THE COURAGE
TO FLY

Stop trying to
calm the storm.

Calm yourself.

The storm will
pass.

DAILY REMINDER

Be a warrior,
not a worrier.

WHEN
THINGS
Change
INSIDE YOU,
things
CHANGE
AROUND
YOU

Better an oops
than a what if

Nothing will work unless you do

MAYA ANGELOU

YOU DON'T HAVE TO BE EXTREME, JUST CONSISTENT

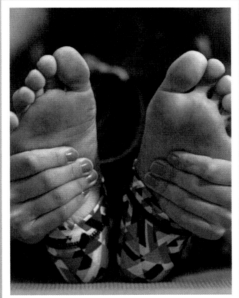

WHETHER YOU THINK YOU CAN, OR YOU THINK YOU CAN'T, YOU'RE RIGHT.

purpose

RELIABLE

innovate

detox

freedom

successful

adventure

CREATIVE

party

wedding

study

I AM	I AM
I AM	I AM

IMPORTANT	SEXY
IN CHARGE	THE BOSS
TAKING CONTROL	RESPECTED
UNSTOPPABLE	INFLUENTIAL

ZEN

Daily Quotes

Make yourself a priority

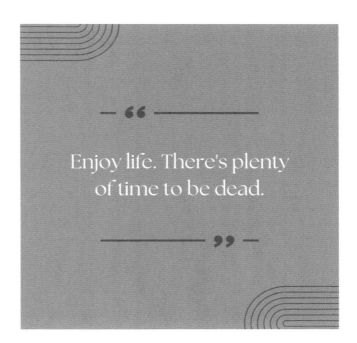

Enjoy life. There's plenty of time to be dead.

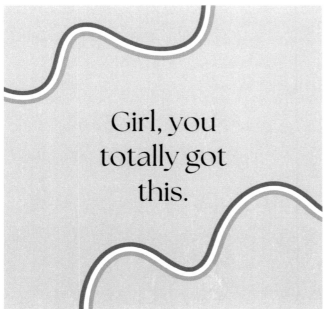

Girl, you totally got this.

JUST BE WHO GOD MADE YOU TO BE

YOU ARE THE ARTIST OF YOUR LIFE. DON'T GIVE THE PAINTBRUSH TO ANYONE ELSE.

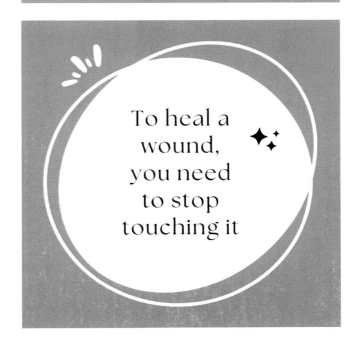

To heal a wound, you need to stop touching it

FINDING YOUR PASSION IS THE KEY TO YOUR SUCCESS

"When I let go of what I am, I become what I might be."

- lao tzu

TOP 5 BUSINESS IDEAS

EVER TRIED.
EVER FAILED.
NO MATTER.
TRY AGAIN.
FAIL AGAIN.
FAIL BETTER.

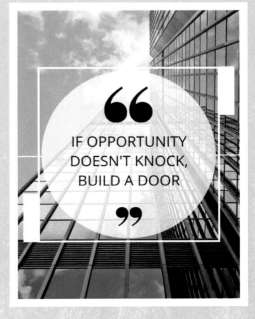

IF OPPORTUNITY DOESN'T KNOCK, BUILD A DOOR

HOME

POSITIVE ENERGY

explore

DREAM

JOY

grateful

connection

GOOD VIBES

meditate

$$$

PEACE

I AM

I AM

I AM

I AM

HEARD

DESIRABLE

ENTICING

ALLURING

SENSUAL

EXCITING

INTRIGUING

INVIGORATED

time to relax

MINDFULNESS

breathe

HYDRATED

EAT MORE VEG

centered

RELAX

ME TIME

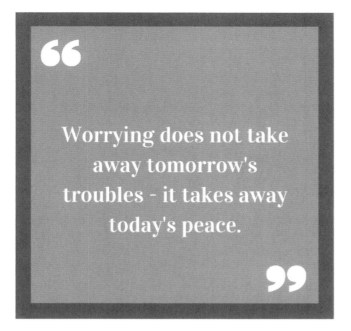

Worrying does not take away tomorrow's troubles - it takes away today's peace.

Not all storms come to disrupt your life. Some come to clear your path.

GOOD MORNING QUOTES

Focus on your goal. Don't look anywhere but ahead

6AM Success

NEVER BE A PRISONER OF YOUR PAST. IT WAS JUST A LESSON, NOT A LIFE SENTENCE

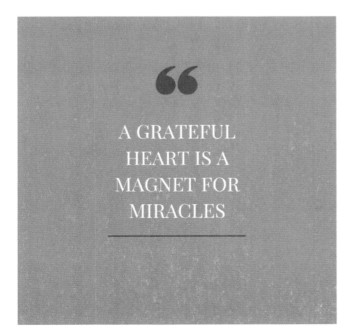

A GRATEFUL HEART IS A MAGNET FOR MIRACLES

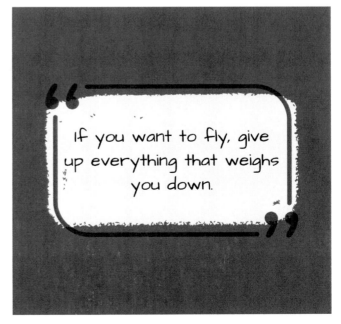

If you want to fly, give up everything that weighs you down.

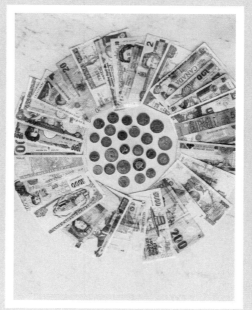

I am a money
magnet

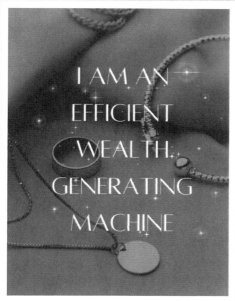

I AM AN
EFFICIENT
WEALTH
GENERATING
MACHINE

I am about to
receive more
money than I
could ever
imagine

FOCUS

PASSION

patience

invest

SAVE

simplify

change

LEARN

BOLD

FORGIVE

Ignite

I AM

I AM

I AM

I AM

THANKFUL

GRATEFUL

SAFE

ACCEPTED

UNIQUE

a divine being

tenacious

KIND

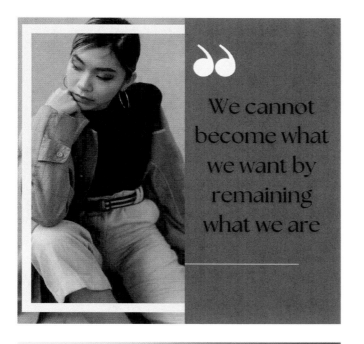

We cannot become what we want by remaining what we are

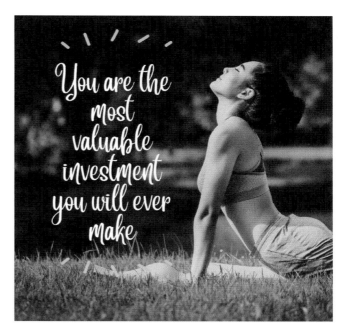

You are the most valuable investment you will ever make

Great things never came from comfort zones

Bad vibes don't go with my outfit

Mistakes are proof that you are trying

Imagine where you would be next year if you start now

YOU DESERVE A LOVE THAT ALWAYS FEELS LIKE SUMMER

REMEMBER

Some things
have to end for
better things
to begin

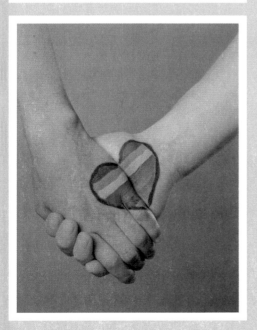

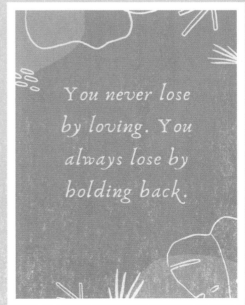

You never lose
by loving. You
always lose by
holding back.

LET GO

KEEP IT SIMPLE

NEVER GIVE UP

POSITIVE VIBES

YES, YOU CAN

IT'S ALREADY YOURS

I BELONG

GOOD VIBES

BE YOU

MONEY MAGNET

PEACE

I AM	I AM
I AM	I AM

spirited	affectionate
courageous	insightful
SMART	open-minded
optimistic	IMPERFECT

Don't be pushed around by the fears in your mind. Be led by the dreams in your heart.

When you focus on the good, the good increases

The comeback is always stronger than the setback

Don't let the concept of change scare you as much as the concept of staying unhappy

I never lose. I either win or learn.

Be loud about the things that are important to you

I have amazing friends

I am worthy of beautiful friendships

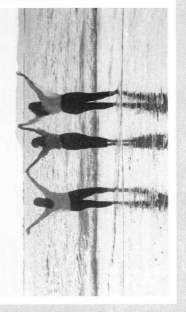

I only attract healthy relationships

Thank you for purchasing this book - we hope you have enjoyed it. As a small independent publisher, your support means the world to us.

If you could leave a review of this book on Amazon we would be so grateful. Positive reviews from wonderful customers like you help other people feel confident about choosing this book. Small businesses rely so much on feedback from their customers and we would really love to know what you thought.

In the meantime, why not check out the other books in our series below. You can find them all at **www.amazon.com/author/ honeybeepublishing**, or scan this QR code.

Other Titles to Enjoy

ISBN: 979-8431856167

If you're looking for inspirational photos of people, places and objects this is the book for you. This book is packed with 600 elements including affirmations and quotes in a variety of categories, all in aesthetically pleasing colors. This book will help you create at least one beautiful and effective vision board.

ISBN: 979-8357605573

Hungry for more? 240 more photos, quotes and words for you to cut out and place on your vision board. Inspiring photographs, creative graphics and ethnic diversity allow you to create a visually appealing and powerful vision board.

FREE E-BOOK

Learn how to use the power of positive thinking and visualization to manifest your goals and desires with this FREE eBook.

Scan this QR code to download your FREE eBook.

THE VISION BOARD
By Gloria Greene

Harnessing the Power of the Law of Attraction to Achieve Your Goals

PARIS

NEW YORK

ITALY

AUSTRALIA

EUROPE

NEW ZEALAND

MALAYSIA

CANADA

AFRICA

BALI

INDIA

I AM	I AM
I AM	**I AM**

- fill in the blanks -

AND SO THE ADVENTURE BEGINS

I am seeing the world

Go where you feel alive